Praise for Serhiy Zhadan's *The Orphanage* (2021)

"A nightmarish, raw vision of contemporary eastern Ukraine under siege from Russian-backed separatists. . . . [Zhadan] unblinkingly reveals a country's devastation and its people's passionate determination to survive."—*Publishers Weekly* (starred review)

"In this novel [Zhadan's] literary talent shines like painful stars over the urban landscape painted by the silence and noise of the war."—Sofi Oksanen, *Literary Hub*

"A vivid glimpse of the current inferno in Eastern Ukraine."—Amelia Glaser, *Times Literary Supplement*

"Powerful. . . . A forceful vision. . . . For those who want a glimpse of what life will be like in Ukraine for years to come, *The Orphanage* offers a frightening glimpse."—Bill Marx, *Arts Fuse*

"With *The Orphanage,* this war finds its bard in Serhiy Zhadan."—Michael Idov, *Book Post*

Praise for *What We Live For, What We Die For* (2019)

"This collection of Ukrainian writer Serhiy Zhadan's poems will likely cement his reputation as the unflinching witness to the turbulent social and political travails of his nation."—*World Literature Today*

"A startling collection of verse."—Askold Melnyczuk, *Times Literary Supplement*

"With this volume, Tkacz and Phipps will whet Anglophone readers' appetites for Zhadan's poetic engagement with a dangerous, polarized, uncertain world. . . . The United States needs a Zhadan as much as Ukraine does."—Amelia Glaser, *Los Angeles Review of Books*

T0038520

Praise for *Mesopotamia* (2018)

"*Mesopotamia* shows the dark sides of post-Soviet life in Kharkiv—addiction, tuberculosis, violent death, rampant crime and corruption—but it also celebrates the reckless joy of young, independent Ukraine. . . . Love and death rolled into one, a booze-soaked multiethnic picaresque."—Sophie Pinkham, *New York Review of Books*

"One of the most astounding novels to come out of modern Ukraine. *Mesopotamia* is seductive, twisted, brilliant, and fierce."—Gary Shteyngart, author of *Little Failure* and *Absurdistan*

"To say that Serhiy Zhadan is a great Ukrainian novelist of whom you might not have heard does not begin to cover it. Serhiy Zhadan is one of the most important creators of European culture at work today. His novels, poems, and songs touch millions. This loving translation is a chance to see Ukraine in terms other than the familiar, but more importantly a chance to allow prose to mend your mind."—Timothy Snyder, author of *On Tyranny*

"Transforming Kharkiv into Mesopotamia, [Zhadan] renders it as a place of irrepressible life and inexhaustible love. And, in doing so, he urges us out and into the world, to be with and for each other. His Ukraine is a republic of love."—Jacob Reynolds, *Spiked*

How Fire Descends

SERHIY ZHADAN

How Fire Descends

NEW AND SELECTED POEMS

Translated from the Ukrainian by
Virlana Tkacz and Wanda Phipps

Foreword by Ilya Kaminsky

A MARGELLOS
WORLD REPUBLIC OF LETTERS BOOK

Yale UNIVERSITY PRESS | NEW HAVEN & LONDON

The Margellos World Republic of Letters is dedicated to making literary works from around the globe available in English through translation. It brings to the English-speaking world the work of leading poets, novelists, essayists, philosophers, and playwrights from Europe, Latin America, Africa, Asia, and the Middle East to stimulate international discourse and creative exchange.

The poems in this volume were originally published in Ukrainian online and in the following collections: *Psalms to Aviation* (*Psalom aviastii,* 2021), *List of Ships* (*Spysok korabliv,* 2020), *Antenna* (*Antenna,* 2018), and *Templars* (*Tampliery,* 2016), all published by Meridian Czernowitz, Chernivtsi, and all copyright © Serhiy Zhadan. For details see the Acknowledgments page.

The Acknowledgments page constitutes a continuation of the copyright page.

Yale University Press books may be purchased in quantity for educational, business, or promotional use. For information, please e-mail sales.press@yale.edu (U.S. office) or sales@yaleup.co.uk (U.K. office).

Set in Source Serif type by Newgen North America, Inc.
Printed in the United States of America.

Library of Congress Control Number: 2023930715
ISBN 978-0-300-27246-8 (paperback : alk. paper)

A catalogue record for this book is available from the British Library.
This paper meets the requirements of ANSI/NISO Z39.48-1992 (Permanence of Paper).

10 9 8 7 6 5 4 3 2 1

Contents

From *List of Ships* (2020)

From *Antenna* (2018)

Foreword

ILYA KAMINSKY

Anyone who has seen Serhiy Zhadan perform with his band, Zhadan i Sobaky (Zhadan and the Dogs), will tell you that it is something to behold. No poet since Allen Ginsberg has commanded such a magnetic presence onstage. The audience goes wild, hundreds of people jumping up and down for hours.

More than simply a rock star, however, Zhadan is arguably the most beloved Ukrainian poet of his generation. Western readers encountering him for the first time might ask, How can such a thing be, in our day and age? How can a poet command such a space, and such a presence, in public life? How can a literary artist also be a rock star, and *also* be a symbol—a civil interlocutor, a public voice of moral authority, a prominent defender of his city in time of invasion, a man who appears on TV discussing poetry even as he daily goes out into the streets under heavy bombardment to deliver food, clothes, and medicine to those in need?

To answer that question, let me provide some context: In the 1990s, in newly independent Ukraine, the people looked to poets for guidance on how to rebuild a vibrant cultural life. It was poets, not fiction writers or painters or musicians, who led public discourse in the arts.

I think, for instance, of Bu-Ba-Bu, a legendary trio of poets who electrified audiences with their public performances. Bu-Ba-Bu, short for *burlesk-balahan-bufonada* (burlesque-bluster-buffoonery), relished the carnivalesque and celebrated the newfound creative freedom in the aftermath of the demise of the Soviet Union. These poets (Viktor Neborak, Oleksandr Irvanets, and Yuri Andrukhovych) often performed to rock music and made appearances at various festivals to wide acclaim.

But the excitement their public performance of poems set to music generated is perhaps the only similarity between Zhadan and the Bu-Ba-Bu generation. Whereas the poets of Bu-Ba-Bu hailed from West Ukraine and were rooted in the Ukrainian-language literary traditions, culture, and folklore of that part of the country, Zhadan is the poet of the post-Soviet landscape, the largely Russophone eastern Ukrainian borderland, notorious for its stagnation and crumbling social order. Writing across literary genres and modalities, he aims throughout his work to give a voice to the forgotten people of the borderland region.

In this region that he calls home, Zhadan searches for language that connects with and makes legible eastern Ukrainians' experiences. The bold, direct negation here becomes an instrument of that connection, a forceful reaching out:

> Just don't call it a language.
>
> Don't call these vines that grow and invade
> the surrounding silence a language.
>
> . . . .
>
> These are anything but languages.
>
> . . . .
>
> These could be the songs of buildings
> from which entire families were evicted.
>
> These could be fonts
> for announcements in newspapers
> burned to heat the barracks.

To speak such a language
is to converse with iron
or argue with linden trees.

*   *   *

Born in 1974 near Starobilsk, a town in eastern Ukraine, Serhiy Zhadan has spent most of his life in the city of Kharkiv. There he published his books, raised a family, and participated as a prominent activist in rallies supporting the Orange Revolution in 2004 and the Maidan Revolution of Dignity of 2013–2014. In one memorable incident, he and his compatriots were stormed by the pro-Russian crowd and ordered to kiss the Russian flag. When he refused, Zhadan was beaten and suffered a concussion. These dramatic historical events have impacted the poet's style: after Maidan, the poet's work took a marked documentary turn. Today, as the full-scale invasion of Ukraine by Russia continues, Zhadan resides in his hometown, supporting his fellow Kharkivites as a volunteer defender of a city under active bombardment.

The spiritual and human landscapes of Ukraine's eastern region, of the post-industrial world where solitary voices search for one another, are present throughout Zhadan's novels, essays, theater pieces, and poetry. He is relentless in his search for speech patterns and registers that can genuinely reach another human:

It's not voices that make up time
but punctuation,
which creates an outline, gives us
moments to inhale and exhale,
mapping out
our connections,
our differences,
our similarities.

Like his poetry, Zhadan's fiction is filled with the paradoxes of a post-Soviet existence, in which people ache for one another and for warmth in the most unlikely situations. It is a landscape where, as his poem "In the summertime" describes it, "two trees stand on the hill, facing each other / like two people who once shared the same hospital room and now meet again." A landscape both raw and somehow impossibly near, where "the sky is like a teenager with textbooks, sorting out the stars, / arguing with the birds, as if they were trespassing." Which is to say, it is a place where lyric strangeness can be found even in the most ordinary instance. This work resonates especially with the generation that came of age in Ukraine during the 1990s and 2000s: these readers see themselves in Zhadan's rendering of the post-Soviet world, in which "winter appears like a book of poems / no one will ever publish," where "waiting for snow" is "like waiting for the war to end."

But Zhadan's writing also manages to transcend his own landscape through his exploration of the dualities and connections between seemingly unlike things. For years he has sought to define the mysterious relationship between war and language. He is a public person who seeks to render visible the most intimate experiences of lovers, knowing all too well that "a language disappears when no one speaks of love." He is a symbol of his country's hope and resistance who has for a long time employed the dual forms of prose and poetry to give a voice to disillusionment, a poet who finds warmth in raw and gritty conditions.

What is a man to do in the middle of crisis?

> So what does this man do?
> He writes poems.
>
> Spreads them out on the table,
> polishes them.
>
> As if getting shoes ready for a child.

The duality of our existence is that even in the midst of crisis there is gentleness, showing itself to us through images of the streets:

> How children embrace the shade like a mother.
> How dogs fall silent, seeing the sun . . .

The tensions between opposites produce sparks; even in the most mundane moment we can find memorable turns of phrase, unexpected tonalities and music. And if it is hope we are looking for, we will find that, too, in this world at crisis, for that too is a duality Zhadan's work encounters:

> And summer will come
> with trains that return to the city
> like fishermen.

All of this, of course, poses many challenges to Zhadan's translators, for they must translate not simply the words, images, and music but also what these images and music *mean* in a very different culture and a very particular historical moment. They also need to find a way to convey the function of poetry in that culture—its impact.

So when I say Zhadan's work has taken a more documentary turn, a reader might perhaps think of Charles Reznikoff's important work making poetry from court testimonies after the Holocaust or C. D. Wright's moving poems dealing with the U.S. prison system or civil rights movement. Or from another perspective, one might think of Tracy K. Smith's erasure of the U.S. foundational historical document to make it into a lyric statement of resistance. These, among many others, might offer surprising and apt parallels, but Zhadan's poetry aims to do something else, in its very particular landscape and moment in time. His aim is to catch the *tone* of his epoch.

Which is to say, Zhadan's documentary chronicles in verse find poetry in unlikely spaces: Soviet-style apartment blocks, concrete streets that look exactly like hundreds of other concrete streets. He writes poetry with a kind of journalistic perspective on locales and people who have been missing from literature, but his documentary mode blends lyricism and irony, even sarcasm, to showcase the tonality of the post-Soviet epoch.

Zhadan consciously tries to bring these prosaic, testimonial elements *into* lyric, investigating the lives of people on the margins of the state, and he attempts to do this not just in the content of the work, but in the timbre and pitch of the voice that says the words. At the end of the day, though, the poet of the people must realize that he is not simply shouting at the crowd of people from his podium, he is also one of the voices *in* the crowd. Zhadan understands this:

> I've seen how birds fall in the snow like schoolchildren,
> when they feel too lonely above.
>
> This happens every time winter arrives.
> This actually happens to all of us.
> It will happen to me too in the end.
> I will come to the lake holding a lantern.

Perhaps this realization is what shows us that a rock star is first of all a lyric poet, one who knows that "music . . . circulates in the lungs of men," yes, but also one who suspects that "the limits of loyalty are still marked by / night music." This knowledge is as heartfelt as it is ironic:

> Poets buried near shopping malls
> make good tourist attractions.
> A poet should be useful even after death.
> Not too convenient alive,
> unpredictable in the theater,

like a stone in a child's hand,
shocking like a bird flying into a kitchen window
. . . .
Cities bury their poets,
like jewelry hidden under clothes.

This perspective is not for the faint-hearted. But I doubt anyone opening a book of poetry by a contemporary Ukrainian poet is looking for platitudes. What you find here is a voice whose language is marked by violence and war:

Listen to me,
you—deprived of the sweet receptors of song.
Listen to me now,
hear my whisper,
distorted by the acoustics of nonexistence.

Even while addressing us, Zhadan admits that it is quite another addressee he has in mind: "I'm most interested in words / used to address / the dead." We have the opportunity—and the duty—to witness a poet in the midst of such a conversation. Perhaps that is why in wartime his public events gather hundreds of people who have lost loved ones and don't know what to do, don't know what language to speak to those who are no longer alive. Breaking bread with the dead is something poets have done for ages, W. H. Auden once told us, echoing *Gilgamesh*. Perhaps with that in mind, Zhadan presses the conversation farther, asking:

What if someone spoke a sentence
that could stir the sonic field of death?

What if someone spoke such a sentence, indeed? May you find many such sentences in this book, dear reader; I know I did.

How Fire Descends

New Poems
(2021–2022)

"WHEN SO MUCH IS TAKEN AWAY"

When so much is taken away
something is always given in return.
Something useful, like the experience of sudden parting.
Where else could you learn about
how suddenly the thread can break,
how suddenly the confused heart can stop?
Pain.
Pain and hope can return your lost sense of this world.
Give life to your essential being, give it meaning.
Pain and hope, which you never expected,
never talked about at family dinners.
Where else can you hear this voice from the forest
frightened by fire, who else can
focus your sight, tune it
like a grand piano, so that your eye won't go flat,
so you recognize the shadowy beast
in the middle of the field?
You survived
the insane balancing act this winter,
collecting fears like old books
from your parents' library,

so now, how can you complain about the weight
of events that have pushed you
into the cold air of history?
Don't you dare,
don't you dare complain
when those burned by rage don't cry.
The mutilated landscape clenches its teeth,
framed by light,
slashed by moonlight.
Pain and hope unite us
in the openings of the dark sky.
Pain and hope, the lungs of a drowning girl,
as the green pond water is forced out,
return her to life.
Pain and hope,
a house rebuilt after a fire.
But in this rift the past retreats,
a shoreline into the darkness,
only in this expanse of patience
can a hint of appreciation appear for what
made you relevant
this spring, so clear, so precise,
set against the sun,
backlit in the wind.
I saw how sleepy women on trains
grab on to invisible voices,
like on to a thread leading them down the corridor.
I saw how fires of inspiration go out over the heads of men.
How children embrace the shade like a mother.
How dogs fall silent, seeing the sun
move over the city.

But summer will come,
with a great scorched river,
and boys on asphalt soccer fields,
like the letters of the constitution,
will testify to the quality of those born on the border,
the quality and honor of people who since childhood
got used to having their skin ripped off by the harsh asphalt;
got used to the pain and the hope,
and stitched up the torn flesh in the thick
light of July.
And summer will come
with trains that return to the city
like fishermen,
let them return with their catch,
let them carry into the cities our hope,
bitter as smoke,
bitter as
writing . . .

July 6, 2022

"REMEMBER EVERY BUILDING"

Remember every building and every street, you tell me.
Remember everything that disappears like a traveler descending
    a hill.
Saying it out loud will drive away the silence and ward off trouble.
Just try to remember this light which pierces the apartments and
    roofs through and through.
Right now—when there is no turning back from September.
Right now—when we embrace as if we were at the wedding of other
    people's children.
Remember these figures in the streets, refined by exhaustion
    and love.
Remember the ability of birds to come together in the autumn air,
the ability to absorb a person's fear and warmth, hidden under
    their shirt,
the joy of recognizing who is on your side by a slight turn of the head.
Despite the wind, remember the breath, the presence, the eruption
    of language.
As you choose your words: just try to remember this month,
which changes everything, these trees, growing like children, easily
    growing into maturity.

September 11, 2022

"OF ALL LITERATURE"

Of all literature
and all language
I'm most interested in words
used to address
the dead.

What if someone spoke a sentence
that could stir the sonic field of death?

Listen to me,
you—deprived of the sweet receptors of song.
Listen to me now,
hear my whisper,
distorted by the acoustics of nonexistence.

Listen to me,
you—marked by dialects, like scars throughout your lives,
you—whose throats were scratched since childhood by the burning
   needles of the alphabet,
you—singers who could imitate bird calls.

I know—it is unfair
you cannot answer
the voices calling out to you from the mist today,
you cannot say anything to defend yourself,
you cannot protect the vacant land of night
between memory and expectation.

But language is important even after death,
like the deepening of a riverbed,
like the rise of heat for the first time in autumn
in a great home.

The only rule—grow roots,
break through.

The only chance—reach out for a branch, grab hold of a voice.

There is nothing else.
No one will remember you for your silence.
No one but you can name the rivers nearby.

You who are only echoes,
you who are filled with silence,
speak, speak now,
speak as grass,
speak as frost,
speak as conductors of music.

"THEY DIDN'T TELL YOU"

They didn't tell you the most important thing.
They didn't warn you that death is limited
by the silence that comes with it,
death does not step out of the chalk circle
drawn on the floor in a room
where all the furniture has been removed
so that the frightened soul
won't smash into it, like a dog locked in the kitchen.

They didn't explain that death is local,
it doesn't run out of the hospital yard,
it is of little interest to anyone
not part of the funeral procession.

They didn't warn you that grief like sonic waves
is transmitted to those tuned in to signals of despair,
who hear the echo of decaying language,
the mechanism of silence.

You do not understand why the living do not unite
when one of us has died; where is the solidarity
of those left behind, or the parting song
that becomes memory?

You think that the writing of death foresees
no transmission. There's only the divide,
no light comes from the other side of the wall.

Life fills everything with itself.
First of all—our fear of death.
First of all—our dependence on experience.

You remain here, you dissolve in this stream,
you are rooted in the pauses of song,
sink into the music of darkness, press into the black letters of poetry.

Everything remains here.
Everything is found between us.
Darkness is easy to read.
Everything has its own word.

"YOUR ATTENTION IS GREAT"

Your attention is great.
Your presence is generous,
you split into light and dark.

As the performance begins, darkness recedes.
The eye fractures the light,
making life incomprehensible.

So you get used to this world, its outlines,
so you begin to perceive things as you see them.
So time appears,
so does perspective.

Mysterious things happen,
the great divide appears—
breath breaks:
inhale—exhale.

The world looks at you with its green eyes.
Looks at you like the stamp of God on a battle flag.
There is nothing in you but light.
There is nothing in you but sound.

A confirmed view of the horizon.
The optics of a bird entering a stream of air.

That's how things acquire meaning.
That's how music starts.
Fog is lost in travelers.
Rivers reflect in fishermen.
Love makes people.

". . . SPEAK NOW"

. . . speak now, or forever hold
your peace, explain the obvious—
how fire descends on lovers,
how despair, like a butcher, can rip out the entrails of the world,
spilling them onto the pavement on a September morning,
speak now, while you can still save
at least one person, while you can still help.

Speak now on what will happen with the next plunge
into the deep current, the next dive into the dark frantic state,
into the depths of trouble, where water like silence
lasts longer than any speech and is weightier than words
spoken in the heat of the moment, stronger than the declarations
of two people caught up in the dance of love.

Warn these carefree folks, driven
like fish by the rhythms of ground water, the changes in
the direction of the wind, the October sun, warn them
that everyone is swept onto the beach, their insides ripped up
by cold broken glass,
no one can stop this current,
no one can read the book of the heavens,
written in the dead language of autumn.

Better to speak now, as the enchanted
count birds, like letters of a name written out
by a child, speak now, try to interrupt

the joy of these adults
who stand facing each other,
guarding their solitude.

The plasticity of the dance of birds in flight,
the logic of the turns of a
warm body, like letters in a
sentence of joy.

Everything is clear from the start.
But has this stopped anyone?
Has it scared off anyone?
The endless churning of a river.
Endless warnings and endless bravery.
They are so strong when they begin their journey south.
And such a sad sight when they return home.

BRECHT

Which poet is buried in this city?
Who lies in the city soil
deep as the subway,
deep as the water pipes?

Poets buried in the city
are like planted bushes
like roots of invisible trees.
What grows from such roots?
Trunk of light, stalks of sound,
an invisible crown of anger,
the inaudible rustle of irony.

Poets buried near shopping malls
make good tourist attractions.
A poet should be useful even after death.
Not too convenient alive,
unpredictable in the theater,
like a stone in a child's hand,
shocking like a bird flying into a kitchen window
from the summer street—
now of benefit to the city,
to the community,
lying in the earth,
calling out to people walking by:

"Step right up, step right up, friends,
let's solemnly stand on the cemetery grounds,
remember, you must remember
at least one poem you heard in childhood.

 "What did I say about you when I was alive?
I called you crooks and thieves.
What did I promise you after your death?
Quiet, peace, and eternal salvation.

"Step right up, step right into the shade.
Think about the kingdom of god.
Believe poets tell the truth,
death is only a draft between floors,
a ray of light on the sidewalk."

The people stand on the old city cemetery grounds,
happy to find a familiar name on a gravestone.
Cities bury their poets,
like jewelry hidden under clothes,
like physical defects.

The people stand under the infinite sky
clouds so high they're almost invisible.
They're disturbed death is so near,
but relieved it has not yet arrived.

"THE MEANING OF WINTER CHANGES"

The meaning of winter changes.
The snow, which we so skillfully avoided,
is almost here—those sparkling mineral flakes
of patience and peace, which we fear,
will descend on bus stops and train stations.

But it's still autumn, and the battle for this city
will be fought till the final round.
I still manage not to see you,
I still believe in your mistakes.
The limits of loyalty are still marked by
night music—wicked and choral.

You still defend your easy pace,
the October wind, the resistance that rises below the skin,
the ability of the syllabic to stretch
the breath, to break the meter—
and put off the essential for later.

We are forever united by nothing,
we must battle the snow like we battle despair.
This is our other world,
the fiery eastern Ukrainian cause,
the concealed faces in the shadows.

We still have to touch the core of night.
We still have to defend Troy in the morning.
You will always be more than a sister to me.

You will always be closer than death.
Destiny that started as a game.

Because you stayed and endured,
because of your stubborn belief in success,
I will stay in the game and mark
the echoes of laughter, the memory of craft,
the feverish chill of biography.

The captured fire still burns.
Today and tomorrow, I chant
your words—unheard of, lordly,
imprecise for defining things.
Night rains touch shoulders.
Night rains the condition of the weather.

And death will come to one in a hundred
and that one will stand and leave.
Let the unseen be with us.
Let the cities that hold out be with us.
It's late autumn. Wars still rage.
The music's enduring and simple.

"I DON'T KNOW WHO KILLED YOU OR WHEN"

I don't know who killed you or when.
I don't know where you are buried.
The world is full of secrets and mysteries.
A border stretches along chalk-white cliffs.

The fatigue with Christmas holidays.
Frost on the Virgin's cheek.
I'm talking with you five years after the fires,
after they fished you out of the river.

You can remember my name.
We're not afraid of death. We're afraid of loneliness.
The point isn't who I departed with.
The point is who you're left with.

The moon is like a stone in a field.
Now the worst thing has happened.
Death is very close, you hear it,
you're just assuming someone else is being called.

You still feel the dew underfoot.
Time leaves its marks on the teachers first.
After five years we grew
as grass on school football fields.

Anger strengthens your shoulders.
Time for proposals, time for beginnings.
When no one answers you—I am silent,
I've become silence itself, in silence.

Silence, which no one can cut.
Silence of unspoken insults.
The point isn't if someone remembers me.
The point is will someone ever mention any of you?

Death is at arm's length.
Eternity is made up of individual seconds.
Deep in the earth the soldiers
are making the warm ground fertile.

Eye of the night sky, eye of winter.
Someone returns to the city, rebuilds their home.
The point is we are talking about it.
That's the point.
The point is exactly that.

From *Psalms to Aviation* (2021)

"THERE WERE WORDS I SAID"

There were words I said about people and their stories.
There were words I called objects held in children's hands.
There were words I tried to use to explain my fear—
fear of silence, the fear of a traveler
who has no one waiting for them at home.

So now I choose words to describe distance,
the space of estrangement, the geography of forgetting.
How people draw apart like air currents.
How breath breaks off at the orchestrated beat of an insulted heart.

I choose words to confirm what we say matters little.
Words to explain how silence slips through these sounds like a fox.
I listen through the night to a woman's breathing like the breath
    of time.
I listen and repeat words declaring dependence and love.

The eye catches a poem like a bird out of the dark grammar of
    the skies.
Catching screams and sighs in dark anthologies.
Be open with me, as open as you are

when parting with those who died too young.
Be tender, as tender as you are
feeding stray dogs.

Cast into a world of bounty before the holidays,
cast there with all our stubbornness,
we learn again the demands of citizenship,
we decide to stay in this country with the language of our fathers.

A short rest for air over our warm homeland.
For the word that makes you turn around in a frightening crowd.
The right to breath is like the right to your own voice.
The start of a book is like the beginning of a rainstorm.

"SOMEDAY THEY'LL TALK ABOUT THIS TIME"

Someday they'll talk about this time as a time when poems
   were written.
They'll say, In those days there was so much air, you had to speak.
In those days air itself was more expressive than any poem.
Fire was more convincing,
more eloquent than silence.

One day, we'll be reminded of this time by the metal inserted
beneath the skin where there was a fracture, at a place of transition
where light reminds you of darkness,
where we see our weakness as courage.

This time will give us poems injected into the breath of men
   and women,
poems that exist in silence, like grass in winter—
it's too late for fear and nowhere to hide from the snow,
only your voice reminds us of thaw in spring.

Someday I will talk about this time as the time of your presence,
the time when you broke into my language, when my world stood
at your shoulders, when the fires died down with your breath,
when fog hovered above the park trees
like warm breath over children running out of school.

We can't forget what tempted us then.
We can't put aside this work on which our breath depends.
We can't—we'll be left breathless, we'll stumble and lose faith
in our trees, our river, the dark pages of our sky.

Now the hardest thing is to be grass.
Now it's particularly hard for broken stems.
Now you turn and start to speak.
I hear you.
I understand.

"YOU WILL NEVER WRITE"

You will never write about how it all really was.
You won't dare, you'll keep it to yourself,
put it aside, keep it in the dark.

You'll talk about literature
when you should talk about life,
that life rushes out into the street
like a dog you forgot to walk.

You'll never admit
what really made you
talk that evening.

Still, what did you risk by pouring out your dark heart,
what did you really want—you won't write about that either,
that's something you won't share.

The fracture that will let the voice appear:
who will light the fires in the lands of silence,
in the lost territories?

You won't write that you didn't believe
until the very end in her willingness
to listen, her ability to understand
the language of stones hidden in the grass.

Here I am.
Here is my heart.
It is not beating.

It is not beating at all.
Don't pay attention,
don't listen.
Time to leave the dark, like a hospital.
Time to give thanks and sing.
Time to come out.
Time to dare.

A fiery ship solemnly
turns in the air above us
and angrily drops in the dark of the night—
time to dare to speak,
time to come out of the night,
time to mend fractures.

Poetry, the most moving and piercing poetry,
poetry reminiscent of a field in November:
you can only guess what was actually meant,
you can only enjoy it
you can only reread it.

"WHEN YOU REALIZE"

When you realize
that when she speaks about you
she no longer talks
about fear,
then you start noticing autumn,
you notice the fire.

A stream,
a great stream of air over the city,
a stream of history
over the building at night.
The woman looks at trees,
examines
the clockwork
of love.

"History, talk to me,
don't let go of my hand,
don't walk away.

"This time of year
it's easier to be together,
together we'll manage,
together we'll overcome the rage
pent up in this man,
who points out doomed buildings,
afterward they burn
with a sacred fire."

"Burn,
burn out of me the desire
to always remain
in her memory,

"burn out of my throat
the desire to rename everything,

"burn my lungs,
like sails of Greek ships,
burn my palate,
like clay."

It so happens
that we are standing right here
between the streams of air,
between the corridors of language.

So that's how clay is shaped,
that's how stems grow,
that's how the music of faith
speaks through us
like intricate flutes.

Only
when you half hear the music,
when you half hear the night voice,
half whispered,
half silence,

only then
loss deserves memory,
fear deserves faith,
breath deserves music.

"IN THE SUMMERTIME"

In the summertime everyone wants to feel the cool touch of the river.
The birds in summer gardens are crazy and unrestrained.
Two trees stand on the hill, facing each other
like two people who once shared the same hospital room and now
    meet again.

The summer is so endless that everything stands still.
The moon rises in the evening over the roadside thorns.
The days are so long that when dusk finally arrives
everyone revels in the dark and doesn't sleep.

The sky is like a teenager with textbooks, sorting out the stars,
arguing with the birds, as if they were trespassing.
The leaves are motionless, the branches silent
as one tree listens to the other.

"TELL ME AGAIN"

Tell me again. What did you say?
"Your words are like broken glass."
What was the last thing? "Never before."
Repeat that. Light pours in. A poem is being written.
What was before that? Say it again. Say it again.
How did it go? "Grass bravely looks up.
I can never do it again." That's it.
Say the same words
as if turning to face the sun. Those words you said then.
The sound of your name. A splash of water.
The voice is a dark thread stitched along the sleeve.
What else? "I feel you, like grass."
Words you don't understand yourself.
That's it: "Try it now, try to understand it.
Try to read it. Translate it."
A gust of cold air appears like gray in a woman's hair.
How did it go? "I now have the words
to talk about silence." The music of pain.
Music born in trees and in earth.
"Nothing else will ever happen. At all."
Warm fields like full notebooks.
Songs that women take out like scarves from wooden chests.
Music that circulates in the lungs of men.
Adolescent silhouettes of sunflowers and garlic.

"FROM NOW ON THERE'S SO MUCH AMAZEMENT"

From now on there's so much amazement
among poets and travelers
as winter's army cadences
roll over the mainland.

These shores, used to suffering,
are bound by laws and legends,
sunken sailors, underwater flowers
that come apart as sad petals.

The first word is the first light.
One day a shadow will cross each shutter.
The army readies chains and saddles,
accepting death for justice and loyalty.

I have a warm home and blankets for the road,
divine inspiration, colds and stigmata;
I have enough stories
to brave through winter,

about defectors and psychopaths,
about late autumn—those who believe that faith alone
   brings salvation.
Everything will change before the first snowfall.
Everything will change before morning.

What you always knew and what you finally learned,
signals, warnings, and interference.
Winter appears like a book of poems
no one will ever publish.

"PEOPLE ARE LONELY"

People are lonely, he says, this was obvious from the beginning.
And their loneliness is most important.
So let there be a time when it's important for them to gather.
And let them call this time winter.

As long as men are kept warm like bears,
as long as women open themselves to books,
let there be a border, a beginning.
Let them call this border snow.

While something unusual takes place,
while I still have some measure of control,
I should give them something joyful yet sad.
Joyful yet sad. Let's say, hope.

"WAITING FOR SNOW"

Waiting for snow, like waiting for the war to end.
Now this is your light—hold on to it and defend it.
Get used to it, embrace it, embrace it.
Only a twig turns dark in the winter

like handwriting.
Men will gather near the lake,
light fires, stare into the flames.
This winter I will remember only you,

twig, turned dark by the cold.
I know the tracks of birds.
I've seen how birds fall in the snow like schoolchildren,
when they feel too lonely above.

This happens every time winter arrives.
This actually happens to all of us.
It will happen to me too in the end.
I will come to the lake holding a lantern.

And your uniqueness, your letters
will be about the slopes on which we stand,
about our souls, about our fires.
This is how I want to remember you.

I will take with me the color of smoke this winter.
You think I didn't want to? I simply didn't know how.
At least I tried. Maybe this is important.
Now these words are yours, embrace me.

How much time each day is taken up with the observation of plants, or what goes on around them, or the light they support, and the observation of birds, on this or that tree with its complex architecture of branches with passages and hiding places;

time to recognize the right of birds to safety and lightheartedness, time to recognize the right of sunflowers to their dry hoarse voices, time to see the logical movement of soil and streams, with the approach of greenery as the light intensifies;

time to pay attention to the transition; turn off the lights after yourself and take what is most important;

time to shut the gate, say good-bye, and confess—warm buildings remain, quiet streets remain, voices remain, which echo for a long time with good-byes and confessions.

"NO MATTER HOW YOU APPROACH THIS TREE"

No matter how you approach this tree
how hard you try to embrace its trunk,
how carefully your fingers
touch the branches—
you cannot contain it
you cannot hold it
you cannot make it rhyme.

"THERE WILL BE WATERS"

There will be waters
that catch us unaware,
which we cannot avoid,
the people standing on a slope say.

What will we take
fleeing from such waters?

We will take books,
we will take our children,
we will take the portraits
of our dead.

But we don't read books.
We don't talk to our children.
We don't remember our dead.

Water, drown
our slopes,
envelop our past.

We will watch you from the slopes.
We will remember
what you hid.
We will mourn.
We will rejoice.

"WE WATCH"

We watch
how perfectly
the leaves fall
from this tree—

powerful and synchronized
in the air like
a choir.

This fall we have no chance
of surviving without loss,
we have no right
to complain
about the inevitable:

if the world moves
too beautifully,
divine design
becomes too transparent.

"WHAT IF WE SET ASIDE"

What if we set aside
the streets waking up in the morning?
There's too much sun everywhere,
too many expectations.

A page of rain, handwritten,
copied out clean,
rhymes with a cool breeze
that we can set aside
for the burning rooms of August,
when we'll have something to remember,
something to miss.

Let me say,
August is so light
because each summer you count who remains
and you notice the absence of those who departed.
A long night crossing
carries travelers to the other side,
while those left on this shore call out after them.

Let me tell you,
it's not voices that make up time
but punctuation,
which creates an outline, gives us
moments to inhale and exhale,
mapping out

our connections,
our differences,
our similarities.

What if the air in the room
keeps our silence,
which we once hid like stolen silver?
Who can figure out
what we didn't say?
Who can decipher the words
that were silenced?

There was too much sun,
too much laughter.
The nights cold.
Our words bare
like women in dreams.

"A LONG SUNDAY PSALM TO AVIATION"

A long
Sunday psalm to aviation.
A song of celebration for so many travelers.
The gates of all cities fly open.
River deltas flood
over the cold northern lowlands.

Workers arrive at the station,
unload from the train,
preparing to construct and set in motion
the snow this year.

The time has come,
someone has declared it winter,
so the chimneys heat up
like tenors warming up their voices,
and worried mothers listen to
their sleeping children disagree
with teachers in their dreams.

Give us air.
Give us our strength.
Open the November sky like a heart.

Here the doors open into late autumn.
Here the dry cold rushes in from the street.
So now traveler,

you must enter a warm home at night,
taking with you the gap between
waiting rooms and transfers.

Feel the coming snow in the air
like an unwritten poem.
Anticipate the metal work
of winter in empty rooms
of light.

The waiting rooms have
long been damp.
For a long time, men who did not make it home
gathered near the heat.
Children sang songs which gave birth to the moon.
And everything was just beginning.
Everything was just beginning.

"THIS IS A GOOD OPPORTUNITY TO BE THANKFUL"

This is a good opportunity to be thankful
for being born in the twentieth century,
for having the chance to see
the borderline of history,
for the chance to walk through crowded train stations
that slowly empty and then fall silent.

You can be thankful for the opportunity
to write letters by hand,
then hopelessly depend on the postman's leisurely delivery,
only to experience the slow motion of the calendar,
its female sensibility.

Give thanks for that particular feeling of time
measured by how many pages you've read
each night.

Be thankful for space,
firmly outlined in pencil, like a button
held tight in a child's hand.

Those who lived through wars and great upheavals,
stand by windows, parting with
their troubles, as if parting with a dying neighbor.

They notice who lived longer,
who won the doubtful honor
of watching their enemy's funeral.

The bright children of the twentieth century
dissolve in the dark, like railroad workers
on a night shift.

In the morning the train arrives at the station.
Dawn greets all those who got off along the way,
tempted by a lamplight behind the trees.
Dawn greets those who exit at the last stop.

Only joy is left behind,
and despair.
The damp mist entwines with
the careless word.

Stay with me, music of the street.
Stay with me, this feeling of victory.
This feeling of justice.
This rhythm.

"JUST DON'T CALL IT A LANGUAGE"

Just don't call it a language.

Don't call these vines that grow and invade
the surrounding silence a language.

Don't call these beastly shrieks
of love a language,
or the chanting apologies to the betrayed,
or the Old Testament laments of politicians
over cities
they will later burn.

These are anything but languages.
These could be the complaints of stones
that lie on the riverbanks,
knowing nothing
about the depth of the river.

These could be the songs of buildings
from which entire families were evicted.

These could be the fonts
for announcements in newspapers
burned to heat the barracks.

To speak such a language
is to converse with iron
or argue with linden trees.

This is not a language that breathes the divination of peace.
Not a language which lifts you into the air
full of smoke and letters.

Long silence, like a thread,
leads us out of burned streets,
silence warm like a lamb in your arms.

We will withstand this wind
without losing each other
in the shadows.

Men and women stand
holding dictionaries in their hands
and everything is clear in the dictionaries,
like in school math books
or Bibles for children.

"IT WILL BE THE SAME WITH THIS BOOK"

It will be the same with this book.

Stand a long time at the edge of a snowy field,
hesitating to take the first step
into the endless expanse of snow, the endless expanse of language,
observing the bird's wing of winter.

Maybe this time you'll manage to cross to the silence.
Maybe this time you'll manage to find the balance between
light and dark.
Maybe this time everything will work out and the syllables will open
the heart of the smallest reader,
like a river in winter.

Taking up the hard task of reading,
I know how hard it is to convince yourself
that it will really help.
I know how hard it is to admit
that what's really important
are the simple things—
breath held because
of a connection of words,
light which comes down from above
because of a melody—
simple things that distract us from
grave illness and tragedy.

So let's try it again.
From the top.
From that place where there is nothing,
but anything can exist.

Books cannot save us,
but we won't be afraid of what we've read.

Poets cannot teach us bravery,
but meeting them should not cause fear.

Let's try it again.
Let's not be afraid.
Hold books in hand,
like birds we gathered after the snow—
not all will fly
not all will return.
Still, you should not let them go.
They should all be warmed.
They should all be equal in the face of death.

From *List of Ships* (2020)

"LET'S BE BRAVE THIS SUMMER"

Let's be brave this summer.
Let's be patient,
let's be generous.
Let's be ready to see death's shadow
in the dry thin figures
of the sunflowers this year.

Who will remember this summer in ten years?
Who will remember the hot lonely sun
in the mornings?
Who will remember how premonition and foreboding,
fear and happiness
took our breath away
in the summer of '18?

The endless hunt for the Lord's timid prey.
The endless inspections of the riverbeds,
the endless breath of the marsh reeds.
These were the pursuits of our unhappy times.
The era of bird catchers
caught
in their own traps.

Who will be the first to see frost on the August grass?
Only you can be so loved
during this hard summer
in these empty cities.
Four captains carry out the sun
to the hospital cemetery.
New times begin,
the harvest of history is gathered.

"JUST WRITE A FEW SENTENCES"

Just write a few sentences.
It's like sorting books into piles, these given as gifts, those half-read,
like discovering bits and pieces that have accumulated in the house.

Just pile together words
that will explain everything,
finally make convincing poetry.

Do you understand that this is about you?
Do you understand that this is specifically about you?
All the craziness in this world is caused by something,
all the reversals in literature are because of someone.
In my dreams I fight whales for you,
I fall in love with buildings and hills for you,
you make the wild geese fly in the fall,
the plants call out to you from the windowsills.

You understand that all this happens
so you can disagree,
so you can furiously disbelieve,
refuse to see the obvious,
refuse to see it,
refuse to see.

But even though
so much time has passed,
I still have to

pause, for a split second, and gulp down air,
to stabilize my breathing, so I don't choke up,
while talking with you about our carefree life.

Time and again walking out into the dark
at night, I hold the door
expecting you to follow.

Do you understand
my attachment to the coins in the pockets of a jacket,
which I haven't worn since last winter?
We may wake up in different cities,
but are still afraid to disturb each other's sleep.
There's joy each time a journey ends.
The army of archangels in the train station square
battles the demon
over the city.

And we will
arrange the melody of loneliness for tenor
and soprano,
and the drowned inside us sigh
for the air that slipped through our fingers.
The world, like a translated text,
will provoke a ton of comments,
making elusive sense,
sparkling with hope.

"AFTER FINDING MY WAY HERE"

After finding my way here, the street
where red leaves lie on stone steps and terraces,
growing warm like children's clothes,
I noticed the early autumn this year.

Noticed the outburst of color on the opposite side, sensed
the bitter smoke, the smoke of freedom, smoke articulated
by the rays of the September sun in empty churches
that look like lungs ravaged by tuberculosis.

The sight of the forest on the other side,
red like outraged workers marching,
the voices of the people walking on the sunny street,
made me realize: how lonely,

how unprotected we feel in September.
Only in September do random trees provoke us to want
to embrace, only in September does a woman's breath remind us
    of the rhythm
of the universe, only in September, when it's too late to
    change anything.

Only in autumn do you grab hold of warmth, only in autumn
do you sort through clothes, like someone looking for
what they want to be buried in, only in autumn do people
    share warmth,
like water at night: too openly, too trustingly.

But we shouldn't be afraid of openness, not at all.
Oh trees, my friends, you shouldn't be embarrassed by your openness.
At least this autumn you shouldn't hide the bruises
left on your throat by loving teeth.

It's September after all, and the water in wells
reacts to weather, like an animal in its burrow.
I will definitely return, I will definitely return to you.
There are only a few weeks left to embrace on the bare stones.

"MAYBE THE MOST IMPORTANT THING"

Maybe the most important thing I've seen
in my life are the stones in the city from which
trees grow. The granite foundation of Scandinavian capitals,
a landscape full of stability and love.

The dubious joy of being a tree,
the dubious honor of holding the spine straight,
while feeling beneath the deadly cold of your homeland;
standing in the wind teaches restraint
and makes you hold on to the hardness like a last hope.

My friends the trees, you have been cast onto stones,
like preachers thrown to the lions,
did you ever regret
you were born here, to this trouble,
never knowing the ease
of Mediterranean shores?

My friends the trees, did you ever complain
about the wind that made you so indestructible?
Did you ever complain about your place,
formed by the winds of your homeland?

We will take everything we can get from life.
We will shout words of thanks to the sunlit skies of our cities.
We will cry with joy
and laugh at the impossibility of changing anything.
We will strengthen our place:
a country cold as stone,
a people warm as trees.

"BETWEEN WHAT WE MANAGE TO LOSE"

Between what we manage to lose
and what we still believe,
there exists a line scratched
by a nail on glass,
a flock of birds offset by the sky.

Time disintegrates
into fox tracks that lead away from the railroad
and the bent spines of milkweed
along the riverbank.

Time breaks like a twig.
There's nothing to fix, no way to recover
the smooth flow of life towards death.
The most serious poetry,
on the knife's edge, started with us,
the syllabics of libraries overtaken by the dark.

Time freezes like a fox during a hunt:
no way to stop the fierce pursuit,
no hope that the tempered blade of time
will spare us.

To fit
between the flash and the blackout
between what you can't return
and what you haven't refused yet,
just exhale:

I love you in that autumn shawl
in this land where the ground is as dark as
ink used to print schoolbooks,
I love this time that fades into winter
chilling the pockets of our peacoats,
I love these trees that look like older women
who've shed illusions like leaves.

Don't say anything about fear,
don't contradict my premonitions,
don't avert your eyes
when you speak to the killers
when the tender and wary skies
are really on fire.

"SO WHAT DOES THIS MAN DO?"

So what does this man do?
He writes poems.

Spreads them out on the table,
polishes them.

As if getting shoes ready for a child.

Just in time
sits down to work.
Gets to the point.

Soon winter will come
and men will take the poems,
sort through them
gently,
like dry tobacco.

And women
will cry over them,
carefully wrapping them
like gold coins.

The value of a poem grows in the wintertime,
especially if the winter is hard,
especially if the language is soft,
especially if the times are
mad.

"HOW MANY TIMES HAVE I HEARD POETS DECLARE THEIR LOVE?"

How many times have I heard poets declare their love?
How many times have I seen women listen to them,
listening as if to a preacher
or a patient?

On the street and at literary evenings,
in front of random listeners,
or in front of people like us who are skeptical
about poetry and love?

There's almost no poetry left.
There are no words left
to smash during a scandal,
like furniture
in a motel room.

There are no lyric poets,
whose words come to mind
when you wake up on an airplane
about to make an emergency landing.

So what is left?
Well, this couple:
under the skies of the last day of winter,
covered by snow and protected by demons.

Here they are declaring their love and creating a scandal.

Creating the poetry of threats,
creating the poetry of tenderness.
Hearts burn fast like stored grain.
The worlds of rented apartments crumble.

It's a good thing that neither of them
writes poems.

It's a good thing that not everything in this world
can be set to rhyme.

"THIS SHOULD NOT BE VOICED"

This should not be voiced, or chanted in the street
under trees, which sway agreeing with each word
they hear.

It should be like a conversation between children
who saw the sea for the first time and are trying to
describe a wave.

What word would you use for the layering of the golden sands
    of compassion
in the river of language, the painstaking hourly saturation of
    heavy soil?

What is the word for the dissolution of rain into a midnight sea?
How does it sound? Like lungs, breathing:
on the edge of silence, beyond the echo.

This is the sound of the voice moving through the throat, a moment
    before it appears,
half a breath from formation. Letters becoming sound,
being shaped to generate a scream.

Let it remain as
drafts of whispers, drawings in the margins,
efforts that lacked conviction.

What I should have said were sentences that soar like
birds from the pages of our books, our attempts with you
to change language, to make it easy to understand for all
who have no words for thanks or doubt.

What we didn't manage to talk through this September
will pursue us, never leave us,
like old fears in the face of loneliness.

What I managed to save for myself, I did not share with
the city's acacia trees, sharp and questioning like children
whose parents are getting divorced.

Time is defined by voice and fire.
Cold draws the border between exile and return.
What's most important begins with
taking responsibility for
what you really believe.

Are you ready?—they ask those who depart forever.
Are you ready?—they ask those who remain.

Flood waters rise in the night.
Language is fortified,
like a coastline.

"SOMEONE TOUCHES YOUR HAND"

Someone touches your hand,
breaking all the rules.
Summer ends.
Honeycombs
heavy and dark, like icons.

Only later will the fear pass of
the startling handshake in the street.
Children grow up in eastern cities
believing in the sun, like scripture.

The Quiet East,
the dark soil
of your fields is like a mourning dress.
Whose losses and loneliness
gave birth to all of us here?

Each scribe and rebel
came to life here
with one religion—the feeling that
later someone will avenge them.

The edges are built into the foundation
of this spacious building.
So much summer.
So much weight.
Again and again.

From *Antenna* (2018)

1

Stories of love begin in the morning,
in a cold room where the two of them
try to look each other in the eyes
in the blinding light of dawn,
not glance away,
not be embarrassed by what they just said,
not regret what they have just done.
When one of them can't stand it,
and who can't stand it? He can't—
he looks beyond her shoulder,
and in the window notices people walking in the rain;
then what appears in his eyes
can be called love.

Stories of love coalesce that very
evening, on the street, when they both get
as lonely as hands
hidden in separate coat pockets.
What's the difference which hand is lonelier?
What's the difference which hand is colder?
What's the difference who is offended?

This is the second day they haven't spoken to each other.
Things are simpler for her, but
look at him.
He is now dissecting their past.
He is remembering all the sins.
Mauling memory
with his fists, like an opponent's liver,
aiming for the most painful parts:
seeking revenge for the ease,
revenge for the openness,
revenge for the arrogance
of looking into the future,
revenge for the arrogance
of looking ahead.

Who taught you to take revenge on yourself?
Who taught you not to forgive yourself?
Where do they teach this bizarre technique of drunken brawling—
of beating your own shadow to death,
throwing stones at your own reflection
in bookstore windows?

He won't answer,
he continues to beat himself up,
fighting the whole world for the right
to hate this world,
demanding the world surrender immediately.

The world would like to surrender.
The world has no reason to resist.
The world is ready to lay down its arms.

But he's not speaking with her for the second day.
And she is not speaking with him for the second day.
And they are not speaking with the whole world
for the second day.
So how is the world to understand
what they really
want?

2

Tobacco Factories

Now I'll try
to retell it in my own words.

So I won't talk about him,
so I won't talk about her.
So I can talk about what's important.

What's important is that no one can resist
the temptation of falling hopelessly in love,
hopelessly and miserably,
no one can resist this pleasure
and face excommunication from love,
from this church, in which we were all once
baptized.

So I don't have to say
any more about him,
any more about her,
I will talk about what is
considered unimportant,
things you can let go.

We can let go
of the ability to cry
when we are filled with joy,

we can let go
of the desire to live when death overwhelms us,
then we can let it go,

but
till the moment when we can let it go,
till then

men will keep falling in love,
like whales who hurl themselves onto beaches
without the slightest hope of return.

And women will keep working
in tobacco factories,
even though the smell of tobacco
can't be washed out of their dresses.

This I can say,
Yes, of course:

let the factories continue working,
let the tobacco be cut,
let it gather in pockets and folds,
I know that no one can let go of anything,
I know that no one can let go of what is most important—
to hurl yourself onto the beach
to hurl yourself onto the beach
to hurl yourself and never regret it.

3

How are poems written?
This August is so hot, it's like
a stone pulled out of the fire.
Stone, how long will it take you to cool down,
how long will your August heart burn?

The air these days is viscous and still.
In the stairways there are rays of light
like the ones on icons in the scene
when Christ starts to doubt.
And no one writes poems.
Look, say the poets, look—literature
is powerless in the face of light and stillness,
no one has strength to talk
when their throat is parched.

At night she approaches her home,
walks into the dark stairway, steps
on the first step.
The air disturbed by her foot
is thirsty, like a wave
that rolls all the way to the other side of night,
darkness rushes toward the invisible shore,
stubbornly holding its breath
disturbing your breathing,
giving rhythm to the silence.

The rhythm of the August sea,
the meter of jellyfish thrown ashore to die,
inhaling iodine,
exhaling poetry,
not to choke on the insults and the joy.

4

An argument starts between them.
What's the argument?—he wants everything to be like it was
and she wants everything to end
once and for all.
Everything should end,
so that there is nothing.
So she wakes up only because
the sun is in the window
and refuses to move till it wakes her.
So every night children return
from the river with white sand in their hair.
So at night you can hear the breathing
of all the men falling asleep
on their sad pillows.

He begs and tries to calm her,
but doesn't understand what she is saying,
or what she wants.

The moon grows fuller each night.
Ahead there's so much smoke and so many rays of light.
Ahead lie all of life's temptations.
The river's anxious chill.
The second month of pregnancy.

5

After two years of silence,
after they carefully avoided
one another,
didn't greet each other with the holidays,
broke off dealing
with mutual friends,
they unexpectedly met
on the street,
and out of habit
joyfully said hello.

So what happened two years ago?
Heavy atmosphere filled with yelling.
A suitcase filled with her torn clothes.
You must talk to the world, she said,
leaving him forever.
You can reach an understanding with it.
You must search for the right words.
It's better not to be afraid to speak its language.

But he doesn't know what to answer.
He has no words.
He doesn't know what to say to her.

They stand,
silent,
no one wants to say good-bye first,
each wants to seem stronger,
than they really are.

She notices—the creases around his eyes
have grown deeper,
from insomnia and grief,
and his fingers have yellowed
from the tobacco,
but his clothes are the same
as two years ago, she thinks
with envy.

She has bright sneakers—he notices—
Her hair is dyed a color so fiery,
you can burn yourself,
and her lips, what lips, he thinks
hot and chapped:
maybe she was kissing someone long and hard
in this wind,
but more likely she was standing on the street
the entire day, even in the rain,
handing out
flyers
no one needs
advertising English classes.

6

Every morning
for two years
he reads her posts on social media

and thinks,
She still remembers me,
she still is talking to me,
she still is writing about me:

when she is writing about the neighbors—she's writing about me,
when she is writing about new clothes—she's also writing about me,
and especially when she is writing about the weather.

What insult and indignation,
when she mentions
a storm.

7

These past few weeks
you can see
yellow-red dying leaves.
The trees stand as if sick with cancer—
now it's clear how it will end,
now you can see what's ahead,
now it is clear that death will win,
but still
it will be forced to withdraw.

To see this gold passing,
to see water flowing by
is the most anxious of times.
A time when you truly
start to love
air.

She talks about
her father's death,
about how dogged and inevitable it seemed.
He is listening and waiting,
listening and waiting
for her to finish,
so he can
finally
embrace her.

8

They stand on the train platform for a long time.
They don't know whether to go their separate ways or stay,
don't know what to talk about,
what to do with their hands.
The sky is dark and still.
Nothing is left of their breaths and words.
Nothing is left of the touch of warm fabric.
The heart pumps berry-red blood,
as if all the waters of the world ran through one river.
As long as everything hasn't disappeared,
as long as the dark sky hasn't disappeared,
then the possibility of sharing remains,
then the possibility of kissing on this platform,
together with dozens of other refugees, remains,
with dozens of those who want
to share something
to leave something behind.
Oh, country with news always bad,
like diseased lungs,
you can only cure yourself,
you can only heal yourself.
Kiss those who don't believe in anything,
kiss those who lost their nerve.
Give them the last of the sweet oxygen.
Give air
to those
who gasp.

9

Cold morning air.
No one on the street except birds.
He stands at the stop, package in hand.
From time to time he warms his frozen hands with his breath,
regretting he forgot his gloves.

The other man drives up in a car,
recognizes him from afar,
waits, then approaches.

The man with the package hesitates.
Should he stretch out his hand?—
instead, he breathes into his fist,
as if to warm it.

Silently they look each other in the eye.
Silently they hate each other.
Cold Saturday morning,
cold autumn air.

Then he can't stand it, hands over the package,
without a good-bye, goes down into the metro,
gradually warming up.

The other man stands there for a while.
He's not feeling the cold—
he's holding a package
with the clothes
of the woman he lives with
and loves.

And here is one more poem
to prove to her that the earth
is flat and prone to disappearing;
music devils make it spin
and saints dance on its surface
when they descend for village weddings.

Here are a few more words
which should change her attitude
about the nature of the divine
and should convince her that
all these
Christmas sales
will end with Judgment Day
when the dead will rise and assume
their place among the living.

Now she can't disbelieve,
now she can't pretend
that she doesn't know
everything will surely change
after this poem,
after one more poem.

What can break locks on hearts?
Only words
turned upside down.
What can enchant love?

Only poems written over
pages of the Bible
that describe the Apocalypse
in detail.

One more winter begins.
One more conversation breaks off.
The beautiful world stands still, awaiting miracles.
You can't convince anyone of anything.
No one believes in Judgment Day.
And no one believes in poetry either.

All the worse for you.
All the worse.

"ALL ETERNITY LIES AHEAD"

All eternity lies ahead.
There will be time to talk about important things.
Sun rays burst through the airy fabric.
Finally he is coming home.
How long was he gone? she asks.
No time to reread letters written long ago.
No time for hesitation or doubt.
Time emerges out of short breaths,
breathless words, naked
shoulder blades, time is joy and wonder.

He tells her about important things,
things that strengthen her shoulders
and make her knees ring.
Time is silence and breath,
the movement of planets, her gestures as she fixes her hair.

Time for insight and fatigue will come,
as will time for hesitation.
But now is not the time to let go
of important things,
not the time to doubt the truth of this light.
There's a time to love and be silent,
There's time to love and listen,
to return, believe, and love.

All of eternity awaits.
The earth circles the sun.
The sea retreats from the corridors at night.
Men's heavy shoes lie near the bed,
like boats left on the shore
after a long voyage.

"TO MAKE IT TO THE COLD WEATHER"

To make it to the cold weather.
To stand between two autumn trees
like between two women:
the weight of the world is nothing
compared to the weight held by a lane of linden trees
that grow cold under the silvery sky
on a November Sunday.

To make it to the end of another
lucky year:
the poems that were written never explained anything,
the poems that were written changed nothing,
not even poetry—
which is just as undecipherable and unspoken
as prescriptions written by doctors:
language, heal us this fall,
heal us from our inability to communicate,
we all have a chance to be saved this season,
we all can escape this time.

Remember the squares with abandoned trees:
the post office against the morning sky,
street dogs turn their heads toward
the autumn sun like sunflowers,
not taking their eyes off its perfection.

Close the open doors,
put aside the unfinished books,
you can only be healed by language,
a language with its complex explanations of love.
Then you will understand frost,
and can separate light from shadows,
oh, woman, like a tree
oh, woman, like a poem.

From *Templars* (2016)

"HOW DID WE BUILD OUR HOMES?"

How did we build our homes?
When you stand under a winter sky
where clouds turn and float away,
you know you must live where you're not afraid to die.

Build walls out of reeds and grass,
dig great pits, hollow out trenches.
Get used to living shoulder to shoulder, day after day.
Home is where they understand you, even when you talk in
    your sleep.

Put stone next to stone, build your home
on this hard, dark dirt,
dig coal and salt out of the pockets of earth.
We all need a roof for our weddings and funerals.

Everyone needs a place they'll miss—that matters.
Water matters more when you miss it.
If you want someone to blame, it's not us.
All we did all our lives was build our homes.

Brick by brick, nail by nail, wall by wall.
If you can stop me, then stop me.
But if you don't want me here,
then you'll have to tear down my home.

In the sun, far from the emptiness,
trees and children will grow.
Dew appears on the leaves after a long night.
We only built to raise the sky higher and higher.

Determining the height,
we filled the language of space with words.
Giving names again to everything,
we called brick brick, nail nail, wall wall.

The voice is given to the strong for singing and to the weak
    for praying,
A language disappears when no one speaks of love.
Nights are not nights without darkness.
Shine over us, black sun, shine on.

"'YOU HAVEN'T SHAVED'"

"You haven't shaved for a long time" you say; "let me shave you."
A razor knows no anger.
A razor knows no regret.
A razor knows no thanks,
a razor knows no hurt.
I know your face, like the blind know braille.

A razor cuts memory like a reed.
A razor pulls you to the bottom, a razor urges you forward,
past the wasteland of wrinkles,
past the sandy dunes of the face,
drawing past the cheekbones—sharp, like a dead man's.

I know your breath and warmth,
I know that place inside you,
where love turns to hate,
I know your skin—dry, like dirt,
I know everything you've taught me.

A razor will never ask why.
A razor draws blood, like the plague into the city.
A razor follows scars, like ship routes.
"It's been a long time since you shaved"—"let me shave you."

You draw the cold steel past veins,
past streams of blood, past the morning hours,
draw past breaths and sighs,
draw without surprise,
draw without complaints,

past rage and tenderness, past joy and grief,
past skies and black earth, past land and water,
past voices and silence, ever deeper.
The thing's not to slip, you hear, don't slip.

No one knows how love works,
what movement gives birth to it, what conversation,
what joy, what fault makes it rise.
But it works, just try to stop it.

Gently-gently moving past veins,
barely touching with the razor,
pausing in space,
with no support,
one step from death,
one step from life.

"THE BOATS ARE LOADED WITH GRAIN"

The boats are loaded with grain.
The dockers have been working since morning.
A woman brings out cold wine,
pours it into a glass.
Glancing toward the voices, she pours
without rushing, filling it to the rim.
Birds fly back from the dunes,
and sheep sleep in the cove.
The ripe grain falls and falls,
no one will be left wanting.
The woman looks out the window
waiting for him to return.
She waits for him here,
he'll come during the day or in the evening.
The sheepdogs bark near the water,
sniffing the tracks of the sheep.
Darkness seeps into the dry wine,
August evenings are so long.
She's been waiting for him
and will continue.
As long as they're loading the grain,
as long as they take it to the sea,
as long as the smallest of the good Lord's
fish continues to swim,
as long as the tired men
later return with their catch,
following the stars
that lead them home,

as long as there's the possibility he might come,
as long as the earth merges into the sky,
as long as the land breaks off near the Azov Sea,
revealing the rich black soil.
The wait lasts and lasts.
The orchard trees grow silent in the night.
The sun is pumped like juice
in the lungs of the grapevines.

"SO MUCH LIGHT"

So much light. Every time. Forever.
The second line of defense.
The fingers of the sun heat the rivers.
Spring comes to the gray zone.

Rain like a buzz cut.
A defrosted piece of the country.
When adults and children leave the zone,
animals and plants remain.

The sky remains like an empty workshop,
the earth is filled with the dead, like stones,
and from May to August the dead
feed the young corn with their hearts.

They water the dry roots with blood,
warm the heart of the earth.
Their lives were so full of suffering
that it remains even after their death.

They came here first and died here first.
The blood on the clothes—only stains.
But even after their death, the dead can
take care of fields and grasslands.

You can see death as grief.
But death always has its own reasons.
Here the dead have done their work.
The trees of the gray zone blossom.

"IT'S ALL JUST LIKE IT WAS A HUNDRED YEARS AGO"

It's all just like it was a hundred years ago.
Time moves in a circle.
The army is loading on trains,
heading home.

Evening shadows intertwine.
Secrets are born.
Once again, the history of our land
is made along a railroad line.

Trade happens here
and news is passed on.
Station roofs hold together
the people of this land.

People stand there with sorrows
they can't shed,
hiding all night at train stations,
like in old churches under siege.

The war has lasted a century,
and will last for ages,
preachers and train conductors
carefully check each face.

The train's packed with all kinds of people
carrying heavy baggage,
bound with silvery wire
sewing together painful deep cuts.

Healing wound after wound,
soothing the rash of the heavens,
holding together the loose black earth
with rails of cold steel.

My dear, my only,
my sweet and faithful,
when the hour is endless,
when tenderness is short,

when there are so many simple things
and even more complex ones.
Nothing changes.
It's a good thing, it's all like it was in the beginning.

Acknowledgments

UKRAINIAN

New Poems

The following poems published in 2022 were taken from the author's Facebook page, © Serhiy Zhadan 2022. All rights reserved by and controlled through Suhrkamp Verlag Berlin: "Я щось обов'язково дається взамін" ("When so much is taken away"), "Запам'ятати кожен будинок" ("Remember every building").

The following poems published in 2021 were taken from the author's Facebook page, © Serhiy Zhadan 2021. All rights reserved by and controlled through Suhrkamp Verlag Berlin: "З усієї літератури" ("Of all literature"), "І не розповіли" ("They didn't tell you"), "Великою є твоя увага" ("Your attention is great"), ". . . хай скаже тепер" (". . . speak now"), "Брехт" ("Brecht"), "І змінюється значення зими" ("The meaning of winter changes"), "Я не знаю, хто і коли тебе вбив" ("I don't know who killed you or when").

Псалом авіації (Psalms to Aviation)

The following poems are © Serhiy Zhadan 2021. All rights reserved by and controlled through Suhrkamp Verlag Berlin: "Були слова, якими я говорив" ("There were words I said"), "Колись про цей час говоритимуть" ("Someday they'll talk about this time"), "Але ж ти ніколи не напишеш" ("You will never write"), "І коли ти почуєш" ("When you realize"), "Влітку" ("In the summertime"), "Повтори ще раз" ("Tell me again"), "І вже віднині стільки здивування" ("From now on there's so much amazement"), "Люди самотні" ("People are lonely"), "Так чекати снігу" ("Waiting for snow"), "Як не підходь до цього дерева" ("No matter how you approach this tree"), "Буде така вода" ("There will be waters"), "Дивимось" ("We watch"), "Що ж, залишмо на час" ("What if we set aside"), "Довгий недільний псалом авіації" ("A long Sunday psalm to aviation"), "Ось і добра нагода подякувати" ("This is a good opportunity to be thankful"), "Лише не називай це мовою" ("Just don't call it a language"), "І з цією книжкою буде так само" ("It will be the same with this book").

Список кораблів (*List of Ships*)

The following poems are © Serhiy Zhadan 2020. All rights reserved by and controlled through Suhrkamp Verlag Berlin: "Будьмо відважними цього літа" ("Let's be brave this summer"), "Просто взяти і написати ці кілька речень" ("Just write a few sentences"), "І лише потрапивши сюди" ("After finding my way here"), "Мабуть, найважливіше" ("Maybe the most important thing"), "Поміж тим, що ми встигли втратити" ("Between what we manage to lose"), "А що робить цей чоловік?" ("So what does this man do?"), "Стільки разів доводилось чути, як освідчуються поети" ("How many times have I heard poets declare their love?"), "Хай це буде не для голосу" ("This should not be voiced"), "І хтось торкнеться твоєї руки" ("Someone touches your hand").

Антена (*Antenna*)

The following poems are © Serhiy Zhadan 2018. All rights reserved by and controlled through Suhrkamp Verlag Berlin: "Історії про любов" (1. "Stories of love"), "Тютюнові фабрики" (2. "Tobacco Factories"), "Як пишуться вірші?" (3. "How are poems written?"), "Тут між ними починається сварка" (4. "An argument starts between them"), "І після двох років мовчання" (5. "After two years of silence"), "Щоранку" (6. "Every morning"), "Ці кілька тижнів" (7. "These past few weeks"), "Довго стоять на залізничній платформі" (8. "They stand on the train platform"), "Холодне ранкове повітря" (9. "Cold morning air"), "А ось іще один вірш" (10. "And here is one more poem"), "І ціла вічність попереду" ("All eternity lies ahead"), "Так і добути до цих холодів" ("To make it to the cold weather").

Тамплієри (*Templars*)

The following poems are © Serhiy Zhadan 2016. All rights reserved by and controlled through Suhrkamp Verlag Berlin: "Як ми будували свої доми?" ("How did we build our homes?"), "'Ти так давно не голився'" ("'You haven't shaved'"), "На кораблі вантажать зерно" ("The boats are loaded with grain"), "І стільки світла" ("So much light"), "Все, як сто років тому" ("It's all just like it was a hundred years ago").

ENGLISH

The poems listed below were previously published in English in the following publications. Some translations have been modified slightly for this volume.

Anthologies

Letters from Ukraine: Poetry Anthology (Lviv: Art Council "Dialogue" / Drohobych: KOLO Publishing House, 2016): "How did we build our homes?"

Journals

Solstice Magazine (summer 2022), https://solsticelitmag.org/content/three-poems-by-serhiy-zhadan/: "You will never write," "Tell me again," "Just don't call it a language"

Loch Raven Review, 14, no 2 (2018), https://thelochravenreview.net/ten-ukrainian-poets: "How did we build our homes?"

Video

Susan Hwang wrote the music, sang, and recorded the translation of Serhiy Zhadan's "It will be the same with this book " as "Psalm to Aviation 58," https://vimeo.com/542125197.

*   *   *

Translations in this book were performed as part of Yara Arts Group's theater pieces *Radio 477!* (2022–2023), *1917–2017: Tychyna Zhadan & the Dogs* (2015–2017), which received two New York Innovative Theatre Awards, and *Ev=Home* (2015), as well as at numerous Yara festivals, art and poetry events such as *Zhadan and Friends,* three of which were also virtual events (in 2020, 2021, and 2022) and can be viewed on www.yaraartsgroup.net.

*   *   *

Translations by Virlana Tkacz and Wanda Phipps were supported by public funds from the New York State Council on the Arts with the support of the governor and the New York State Legislature. Tkacz and Phipps were awarded the Modern Language Association Lois Roth Certificate for their translation of Serhiy Zhadan's poetry in 2021. Virlana Tkacz was also awarded a National Endowment for the Arts Poetry Translation Fellowship for her work with Wanda Phipps on Serhiy Zhadan's poetry.

*   *   *

The translators would like to thank Julian Kytasty, Olena Jennings, and all the actors who worked on our poetry readings and theater shows for their assistance, especially Sean Eden, Marina Celander, Chris Ignacio, Maria Pleshkevich, Maksym Lozynskyj, Susan Hwang, and Bob Holman.

SERHIY ZHADAN is an internationally renowned Ukrainian poet and novelist. He was born in the Luhansk Region of Ukraine and educated in Kharkiv, where he lives today. He helps organize local artists and musicians as volunteers delivering humanitarian aid in Kharkiv. He is the award-winning author of sixteen books of poetry as well as numerous prose works, and his books have been translated into over thirty languages. In 2022, Zhadan was awarded the Hannah Arendt Prize for Political Thought, as well as the Peace Prize of the German Book Trade for his "outstanding artistic work and his humanitarian stance with which he turns to the people suffering from war and helps them at the risk of his own life." He is the front man for the band Zhadan and the Dogs.

VIRLANA TKACZ and WANDA PHIPPS have received the Agni Poetry Translation Prize, the National Theatre Translation Fund Award, and fourteen translation grants from the New York State Council on the Arts. Their translations have also appeared in many literary journals and anthologies and are integral to the theater pieces created by Yara Arts Group (www.yaraartsgroup.net).

VIRLANA TKACZ heads the Yara Arts Group and has directed forty original shows at La MaMa Experimental Theatre in New York, as well as in Kyiv, Lviv, Kharkiv, Bishkek, Ulaanbaatar, and Ulan Ude. She received an NEA Poetry Translation Fellowship for her translations with Wanda Phipps of Serhiy Zhadan's poetry. She is the author of the book of poems *Three Wooden Trunks* (2022).

WANDA PHIPPS is the author of the books *Mind Honey, Field of Wanting: Poems of Desire,* and *Wake-Up Calls: 66 Morning Poems.* She is the recipient of a New York Foundation for the Arts Poetry Fellowship. Her poems have appeared in over one hundred literary magazines and numerous anthologies.

ILYA KAMINSKY was born in Odesa, former Soviet Union, in 1977, and arrived in the United States in 1993, when his family was granted asylum by the American government. He is the award-winning author of *Deaf Republic.* His work has won the *Los Angeles Times* Book Award, the National Jewish Book Award, the Whiting Award, and the Metcalf Award of the American Academy of Arts and Letters, and it has been shortlisted for the National Book Award, National Book Critics Circle Award, and the Neustadt International Literature Prize, among other awards.